Delight

A WALK THROUGH
THE PSALMS

PSALMS 1-30

by

KRISTIN SCHMUCKER

STUDY CONTRIBUTORS

Designer:
MICHELE YATES

Editor:
MELISSA DENNIS

Contributing Author:
SARAH MORRISON

www.thedailygraceco.com

Study Suggestions

Thank you for choosing this study to help you dig into God's Word. We are so passionate about women getting into Scripture, and we are praying that this study will be a tool to help you do that. Here are a few tips to help you get the most from this study:

• Before you begin, take time to look into the context of the book. Find out who wrote it and learn about the cultural climate it was written in, as well as where it fits on the biblical timeline. Then take time to read through the entire book of the Bible we are studying if you are able. This will help you to get the big picture of the book and will aid in comprehension, interpretation, and application.

• Start your study time with prayer. Ask God to help you understand what you are reading and allow it to transform you (Psalm 119:18).

• Look into the context of the book as well as the specific passage.

• Before reading what is written in the study, read the assigned passage! Repetitive reading is one of the best ways to study God's Word. Read it several times, if you are able, before going on to the study. Read in several translations if you find it helpful.

• As you read the text, mark down observations and questions. Write down things that stand out to you, things that you notice, or things that you don't understand. Look up important words in a dictionary or interlinear Bible.

• Look for things like verbs, commands, and references to God. Notice key terms and themes throughout the passage.

• After you have worked through the text, read what is written in the study. Take time to look up any cross-references mentioned as you study.

• Then work through the questions provided in the book. Read and answer them prayerfully.

• Paraphrase or summarize the passage, or even just one verse from the passage. Putting it into your own words helps you to slow down and think through every word.

• Focus your heart on the character of God that you have seen in this passage. What do you learn about God from the passage you have studied? Adore Him and praise Him for who He is.

• Think and pray through application and how this passage should change you. Get specific with yourself. Resist the urge to apply the passage to others. Do you have sin to confess? How should this passage impact your attitude toward people or circumstances? Does the passage command you to do something? Do you need to trust Him for something in your life? How does the truth of the gospel impact your everyday life?

• We recommend you have a Bible, pen, highlighters, and journal as you work through this study. We recommend that ball point pens instead of gel pens be used in the study book to prevent smearing. Here are several other optional resources that you may find helpful as you study:

• www.blueletterbible.org This free website is a great resource for digging deeper. You can find translation comparison, an interlinear option to look at words in the original languages, Bible dictionaries, and even commentary.

• A Dictionary. If looking up words in the Hebrew and Greek feels intimidating, look up words in English. Often times we assume we know the meaning of a word, but looking it up and seeing its definition can help us understand a passage better.

• A double-spaced copy of the text. You can use a website like www.biblegateway.com to copy the text of a passage and print out a double-spaced copy to be able to mark on easily. Circle, underline, highlight, draw arrows, and mark in any way you would like to help you dig deeper and work through a passage.

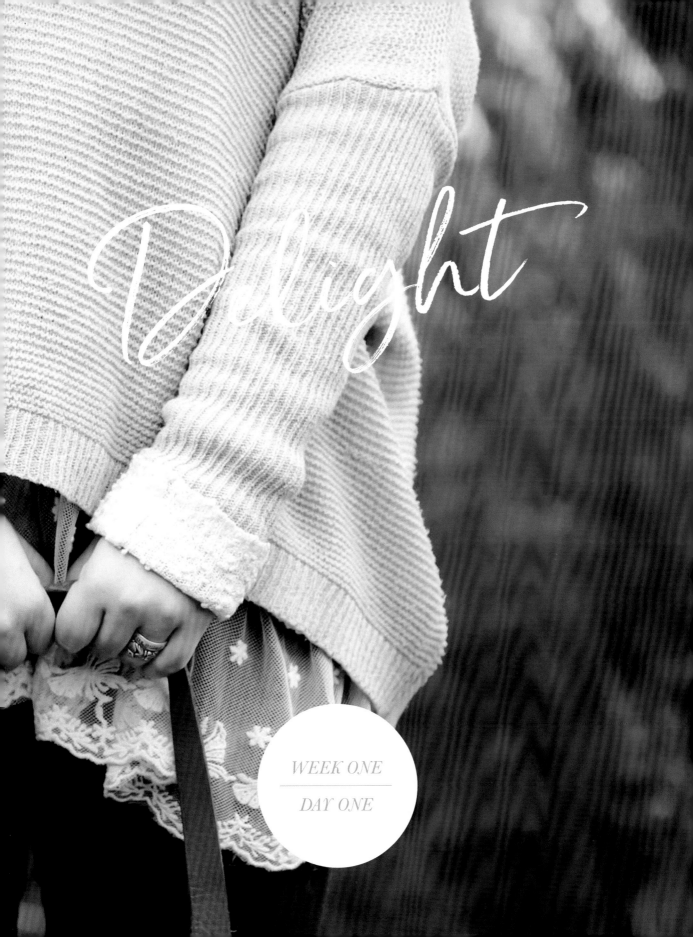

Delight

Psalm 1

The Psalms open with a psalm of wisdom and a contrast of the righteous and the wicked. Some have even suggested that the start of the psalm is as much a description of Jesus as it is an admonition to us to live like Him. The psalm opens like the Sermon on the Mount (Matthew 5) with the word *blessed*, and the psalmist will describe the blessed, or righteous, person for us. We first see what the blessed man does not do. He does not dwell with sinners or become accustomed to sin. Walk, stand, and sit show us a progression of how we can get comfortable with our sin and the sin of this world. At first one simply walks by sin and takes a glance, then one stands near wickedness, and soon one will find themselves sitting down and fully comfortable with unrighteousness. Sin is a slippery slope, so we must stay far from it.

The blessed one delights in God's Word and finds their strength from God alone. They also meditate on it. The Hebrew here gives the sense of constantly meditating. God's Word should be always on our minds so that it can penetrate our hearts. The righteous are like trees planted by the living water. These are not wild trees that grew wherever the wind laid seed, but these are chosen trees, intentionally planted and cultivated, just as we are by our loving Father. These verses call us to abide (John 15) as we see that this tree brings forth fruit in season, and its leaf does not wither. This tree is fruit-bearing and evergreen. The seasons of life come and each season brings new fruit. Even the darkest seasons produce fruit in the life of the believer.

The righteous person prospers in all that he does. We may not think that in what we have done we have prospered, but even our failures are prosperity in God's economy, because He is working them for our good (Romans 8:28).

Just as Jesus reminded us in Matthew 5, God views things differently than this world. This success is measured by God's standards and not our own. The wicked pictured here is the opposite of the righteous, but this is our mission field, those that do not know the hope that we have found and that has found us.

May we be like Jesus. May we be like the Righteous One who delights in God's Word, meditates on it all day long, abides in the Lord, bears fruit, and prospers in all. Not because of anything that we have done, but because of the power of our God in us.

How happy is the one who does not
walk in the advice of the wicked
or stand in the pathway with sinners
or sit in the company of mockers!
Instead, his delight is in the
Lord's instruction, and he meditates
on it day and night.

Psalm 1:1-2

What does it mean to delight in the law of the Lord? In what ways do you delight in the Lord's instruction to you?

Think about what it means to be "planted by streams of water." Do you find yourself "planted" near the life-giving waters of God's Word?

In what ways does this psalm encourage you to live a righteous and holy life?

Refuge

Psalm 2

Psalm 1 began with a contrast of the righteous and the wicked, and Psalm 2 shows us the Righteous One and the wickedness of the world but also the blessing for those that trust in Jesus. This psalm is the first messianic psalm, and it is quoted or referenced in the New Testament at least 18 times. No other psalm is quoted this much, so we can be sure that the message is an important one.

This psalm shows the world system opposing our God and the Anointed One (Jesus, the Messiah). This concept is not a new one. From the beginning of the earth, man in his pride has been guilty of opposing the Lord. However, we are reminded that though the world comes against our God, the battle is already won, and Jesus is the Victor. Though man rebels, God will reign victorious. From the beginning man has rebelled, and yet God has extended mercy for those who would turn to Him.

Here the psalmist gives a beatitude for those that will trust and find refuge in the Lord. Those that reject the Lord will face judgment, but there is grace and mercy for those that place their faith in the King of kings. Our sovereign God is just and holy, and also merciful and loving. We stand in awe of who He is and the grace that has been lavished on us as His people.

Our sovereign God is just and holy, and also merciful and loving

How does verse 1 give you insight into the results of the fall and sin entering into the world?

Does this psalm grow your confidence in the Lord, that He is sovereign and will always enact justice?

Meditate on the line: "Blessed are all who take refuge in him." Do you take refuge in the Lord? Spend some time in prayer, asking that God would continually teach you to take refuge in Him.

Help
for the
Helpless

Psalm 3

Our God is help for the helpless. Psalm 3 is a psalm of David written when David was fleeing from his son Absalom as Absalom sought to take over the kingdom and kill David. David came boldly to the Lord and poured out the burdens of his heart. David was facing many foes, and by the world's standard, there was no hope for him. People looked at him and thought that not even God could help David. But these people must not have known our God. Our God is the help of the helpless, and the impossible is possible with Him (Matthew 19:26, Jeremiah 32:17). David chose to place his trust in the Lord who had made an everlasting covenant with him (2 Samuel 7). He knew that the Lord would keep His promises.

David proclaimed the truth of who God is, and he trusted God for victory. David proclaimed that God was a shield about him. In the original Hebrew during the time period that this was written, the word for "shield" is much deeper than what we know of the word today. It conveys a surrounding on all sides. It was not just a shield in front but a piece of armor that surrounded every side of a soldier. It reminds us that we are being protected from every side. Protected from the enemy on the outside and all the problems of life. We are even protected from the inside and from our own minds and hearts within us that do not always align with the truth. He is our shield on *every* side.

The same God that was with David is with us as well. We can be assured of victory because of who He is. We know that He will keep His promises, and we can rest in His protection. We can live in the victory that only He can give.

How does understanding David's circumstance with Absalom help you to better understand the meaning of this psalm?

In what ways does this psalm bolster your confidence that God will prevail in difficult circumstances?

Dwell on verse 5. In what ways have you experienced the Lord sustaining you?

Answer me When I Call

Psalm 4

Psalm 4 is often called the evening psalm to complement the morning psalm of Psalm 3. The psalm begins with David coming to the Lord and pleading with God to not only hear but to answer. David pleads on the basis of who God is and all that He has done. We can learn much about prayer by observing the psalms. David uses the title, "O God of my righteousness," which is only used in this psalm and gives God the glory for any good that is in David. David remembers God's past faithfulness to him which gives him confidence to trust the Lord. Charles Spurgeon said, "He will never cease to help us until we cease to need." We can be confident that the Lord has chosen us, that He will see us through, and that He will hear us when we call to Him. Whatever we face, we can stand in confidence before men because we have first faced our God. Other people may come against us, but we must be sure to keep our hearts pure before the Lord.

The favor of God and the joy that He gives is better than anything that this world has to offer. Nothing in this world satisfies like Jesus. In 1632 Alexander Grosse wrote, "Where Christ reveals himself there is satisfaction in the slenderest portion, and without Christ there is emptiness in the greatest fullness." The words are just as true today as they were generations ago when they were written. Jesus is the only one that satisfies. He is the only one that brings joy and the only one that gives rest and peace. With Jesus we can say, "It is well with my soul."

Nothing in this world satisfies like Jesus

Meditate on verse 3. What does it mean that God has "set apart the godly for himself," and what does that look like?

Reread verse 4. In what ways can you be angry and not sin?

How does verse 8 grow your understanding of God? Do you trust in the security He provides?

I Will Wait

WEEK ONE
———
DAY FIVE

Psalm 5

In the fifth psalm, we see an urgent and expectant prayer from David. We are not given any insight into the exact situation during which the psalm was written, but it is clearly a difficult time for David. Perhaps, as in Psalms 3 and 4, he is fleeing from Absalom, or perhaps something different. Whatever the case may be, we see David here with a troubled heart.

David comes to the Lord with urgency and asks the Lord to hear him and answer his requests. When he asks God to consider, he is asking God to hear his prayer and then do what is best. We should come to the Lord in the same way. We should pour out our hearts and our requests before the Lord, and then ask Him to do what is best. We must recognize like David that we do not always know what is best for ourselves, but the Lord always knows what is best for us.

David also came expectantly. He believed the Lord would answer. In verse 3, David sets out his prayer as a sacrifice to the Lord, and then watches and waits expectantly for an answer. David calls for God's justice and holiness to prevail against sin and points out that we come to God based on His mercy and not our own merit. We can come to God because of Jesus (Hebrews 10:19-20). Like David, we must recognize that it is His mercy that has delivered us, and then we plead for His way and not our own way. We want His will to be done and not our own will. His kingdom, not our kingdoms. And after we have prayed to Him, we can rejoice because the Lord blesses the righteous with favor like a shield that surrounds on all sides. No matter what enemy we have, we know that our God will go with us.

*Pay attention to the sound of my cry,
my King and my God, for I pray to you.*

Psalm 5:2

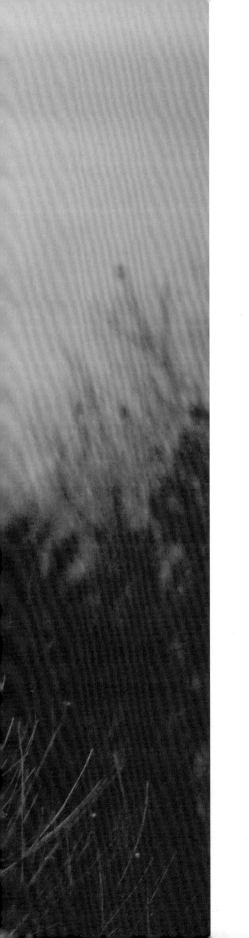

What can you learn about praying expectantly from this psalm?

In verse 8, David asks God to lead him in His righteousness. Why might that attitude be important? Spend some time in prayer, asking that God would lead you in His righteousness.

Meditate on verse 11. What are some reasons that the Lord's refuge is worthy of rejoicing? Spend some time in prayer, praising God for His goodness and for providing you with refuge.

FOR YOU ARE NOT A GOD WHO *DELIGHTS* IN WICKEDNESS; EVIL CANNOT *dwell with you.*

Psalm 5:4

WEEKLY REFLECTION

Read Psalms 1-5

- Paraphrase the psalms from this week.

- What did you observe from this week's text about God and His character?

- What do these psalms teach about the condition of mankind and about yourself?

- How do these psalms point to the gospel?

- How should you respond to these psalms? What is the personal application?

- What specific action steps can you take this week to apply the passage?

The Lord Has Heard My Plea

Psalm 6

Psalm 6 is considered to be the first of the Penitential Psalms. We are not sure exactly at what point in David's life it was written, but it is clear that he was very distressed. David pleads with God to not discipline him in anger, but Hebrews 12:5-11 reminds us that God only ever disciplines out of love. His correction, as a loving Father, is always meant to grow and mature us. David pleads his own weakness and God's infinite strength which is a good plea for us as well. At the end of verse 3, David cries, "How long Lord?"

Certainly there have been times in our own lives when we have felt the same ache. Times when we have felt that ache in our hearts of uncertainty. But our God knows exactly how long our trials will last. He will not allow us to suffer even one day too long. Our God always shows up at just the right time. He delivered Israel from Egypt on the very day He had appointed (Exodus 12:41). He sent Jesus for us at the right time (Romans 5:6-8). He delivered David at the right moment. *And He will do the same for us.* David's emotions were telling him many things, but the truth of God's Word never changed. Through much of this psalm, David is distressed. But by the last three verses something has changed, and David knows that he has not been forgotten and God has heard his prayers.

We serve the same great God that David did. He is working behind the scenes in ways that we do not know and could never comprehend. He will be faithful. He will hear our cries. And at just the right time, He will deliver us.

He will be faithful. He will hear our cries.

What does this psalm teach you about the character and nature of God?

Meditate on verse 9. In what ways does this verse encourage you to run to the Lord in prayer? Does this verse change your attitude or perception of prayer?

Spend some time in prayer, asking that God would grow your confidence that He hears your prayers and that His steadfast love would continue to deliver you from suffering.

Deliver Me

WEEK TWO

DAY TWO

Psalm 7

Charles Spurgeon has called this psalm "The Psalm of the Slandered Saint." This psalm of David is his response to false accusations made against him. The song was sung because of the words of Cush who was a man who flattered Saul and slandered David. When we find ourselves in a situation where falsehoods are being told about us, we can find comfort in these words. We must remember that when we are wrongly accused, God is our refuge. No matter what life brings, we can run to Him for help and strength. He will *never* fail us.

In verses 3-5, David pleads his innocence while also checking his heart and showing his humility before the Lord. Beginning in verse 6, we see David plead with the Lord to "arise" and take action against the enemies. Our God will work on our behalf. Luke 18:7 tells us that He will give justice to the elect. David didn't take the situation into His own hands, but he placed it into the Lord's hands. David's words are a reminder for us to do the same. We can trust the Lord to work for us. The indictment of the wicked is great, and judgment is promised for those that reject the Lord. Sin always catches up to a person. We will reap what we sow (Galatians 6:7).

The end of the psalm concludes with praise to the one who delivers the believer from every attack of the enemy. We can praise Him because we know that He will be faithful to us. He is our Deliverer.

I will thank the Lord for his righteousness;
I will sing about the name of the Lord Most High.

Psalm 7:17

Think about the way that David searches himself in verses 3-5. What does this teach you about humility? Are you willing and able to search yourself for sinfulness?

Focus on verses 8-11. What do these verses say about God as judge? Do you trust in the Lord's righteous judgement? Do you believe that He is perfectly just?

In verse 17, David commits to praise the Lord because He is worthy to be praised. How does this encourage you to praise God because He is good during times of persecution and suffering?

Our God

Psalm 8

He is higher. He is majestic. And His ways are greater than we could even imagine – yet He loves us. The beauty of Psalm 8 is the beauty of the gospel. The perfect God of heaven came down to earth and died for sinful men that we might partake in His righteousness (2 Corinthians 5:21). The psalm begins and ends the same – with the psalmist overwhelmed and in awe of the majesty and glory of God. And yet from the start, we see the sweet truth that this sovereign God of Creation is *our* God. He is high above us, and yet He is personal.

Though He is great, even little children can praise Him and see the enemy defeated. From Moses in a basket to young Samuel to David and Goliath, Scripture is full of accounts of young people. But it would be a young baby in a manger that would come and defeat the enemy and bring salvation. We are like grains of sand compared to the universe, and yet *He* has loved us. He has chosen us in Him before the foundation of the world (Ephesians 1:4). As we look or consider the heavens and all that is created, we can't help but be overwhelmed that He chose us.

"The work of your fingers," gives the connotation of a skilled embroiderer, or the artisan of a tapestry. *We* are the work of His fingers as well. Like the intricate weaving of a fine tapestry, carefully and skillfully crafted together, we are the work of His hands. We see only the back of the tapestry, with messy strings and pieces that don't make sense. But He sees the front and the beauty of the finished tapestry. He is higher (Isaiah 55:8-9), and yet He looks on us. We may not always understand what He is doing, but we can trust His skilled hand.

Meditate on verse 2. What does it say about God's strength and character that He uses the mouths of infants to accomplish His plans?

Observe the work of the Lord's fingers both in nature and in yourself. How does the details and intricacies of what you identify teach you about the character of God?

After reading this psalm, do you find that your ability to praise God has grown? Spend some time in prayer, praising God for His majesty and goodness.

We Will Praise

WEEK TWO

DAY FOUR

Psalm 9

With everything I am, I will praise His name. And He will be faithful. Psalm 9 is a psalm of praise to a God who never fails His people. This psalm gives us a confidence in the character of our God. This psalm of David begins with the psalmist thanking God and praising His name with his whole heart. Verse 1 reminds us of how we should think on all God has done and remember His deliverance. We should remember all of His wonderful deeds, and truly all of His deeds are wonderful, even the ones that we do not understand.

As we reflect back on His faithfulness to us, our praise will continue because He has sovereignly done all things for our good. Verse 2 reminds us that the people of God should be happy people known for our joy no matter what may come. God has defeated David's enemies, and He will be with us as well. Verses 7-8 look forward to the future victory, and we can have confidence in the future, because of God's unwavering faithfulness to us in the past. Verses 9-10 are the heart of this psalm. The reminder that our God will not forsake us gives us faith to face whatever lies ahead.

As the people of God we will never be forsaken. In this world we may feel forgotten or lonely, but the One who has given His own life for us will never forsake us. We cannot help but praise Him and share with those around us all that He has done for us. We share the message that though He is the Just One, He is also the Justifier. We share that though we are weak, He is strong, and that we are *never* forgotten. And then we praise Him for who He is and let the joy of our salvation shine out as a light in a dark world.

The One who has given His own life for us will never forsake us

The first two verses of this psalm denote an active choice that David commits to make—he will give thanks. Are you able to praise God amid difficulty? Spend some time in prayer, asking that God would grow your thankfulness and faith in Him.

Meditate on verses 9 and 10. What does it mean that the Lord is a stronghold? Do you trust that the Lord will always protect you?

Reread verse 14. What does it mean to rejoice in God's salvation? How does rejoicing in God's salvation give us a proper understanding of the trials we suffer on earth?

He Sees

WEEK TWO

DAY FIVE

Psalm 10

Our God will never forsake His own, and we can praise Him right in the midst of this life. This psalm does not indicate it's author though it is commonly believed to be a psalm of David and a continuation of Psalm 9. The psalm opens with a plea of why the Lord had hidden Himself. The beauty of David is not that he was without struggle but that he ran to God again and again. He allowed his struggles and even his own sin to only draw him closer to the Father. The Lord never leaves His people, and in the moments when He seems distant, we can take comfort that He will walk through the fire with us. Hidden but still present. There may be times when it seems to us that He has hidden Himself, and we do not understand His plan. And yet even then we can know that He is still there.

This psalm describes the wicked. The description shows their many sins, but all are rooted in pride. Our sin is also rooted in pride and a deeper love for ourselves than for God. Pride keeps us from seeking the Lord (v4), and the wicked are characterized by living as if there is no god but themselves. Lord, let it not be true of us.

In verse 12, the psalmist cries out to God in prayer. Two different Hebrew names of God are used here. "LORD" here is Jehovah or Yahweh, the covenant name of God. God is "el" which means strength, might, or almighty. The psalmist is praying for God to rescue in all of His attributes. The psalmist is praying, *O LORD, keep your covenant and promises to me. O God Almighty, rescue me in your mighty strength.* The psalmist comes boldly in faith, and we can as well (Hebrews 4:16). We are pleading on the basis of who He is, and as we cry out to Him our hearts are reminded that He is faithful, and He will be faithful to us as well. The psalm ends with a song of thanksgiving for all He has done, all He will do, and for who He is. This faithful, covenant keeping, almighty God hears the cries of His people.

We come in prayer not to plead our case, but to plead His character. We cry out to Him, *Lord, You are faithful, be faithful to me. Lord, You are the comforter, comfort me.* He has been faithful in the past, and we can be sure that He will be faithful again.

Lord, you have heard the desire of the humble; you will strengthen their hearts. You will listen carefully, doing justice for the fatherless and the oppressed so that mere humans from the earth may terrify them no more.

Psalm 10:17-18

Reflect on some instances in your life where God might have felt far away. How does this psalm bring clarity to such situations? Do you trust that the Lord will not forsake you?

Reread verse 17. In what ways does this verse give you hope and comfort in the character of God?

Think about what it means to "plead the character" of God in prayer. As you read this psalm, spend some time in prayer praising God for His good character and the attention He gives to those in distress. Plead His character.

I WILL THANK THE LORD WITH *all my heart;* I WILL DECLARE ALL YOUR *WONDROUS WORKS.*

Psalm 9:1

WEEKLY REFLECTION

Read Psalms 6-10

- Paraphrase the psalms from this week.

- What did you observe from this week's text about God and His character?

- What do these psalms teach about the condition of mankind and about yourself?

- How do these psalms point to the gospel?

- How should you respond to these psalms? What is the personal application?

- What specific action steps can you take this week to apply the passage?

We Will Trust

WEEK THREE

DAY ONE

Psalm 11

Faith > Logic. In this psalm, David is in a bad situation. He is likely fleeing from Saul who was seeking to take his life. It was a serious time, and this psalm is a psalm of confidence in the Lord. Our situations so often sway our emotions and even our trust in the Lord, but David reminds us in this psalm that even when the situation seems hopeless and logic would tell us to throw in the towel, even then we must trust the Lord. This psalm reminds us that we walk by faith, and not by sight (2 Corinthians 5:7).

When we look at our own situations, it seems hopeless. But our God sees what we cannot see. Every part of our lives is a part of His sovereign and perfect plan. We see our lives as a series of good and bad things, but His perspective is not our perspective. *He sees what we do not see.* And He can take the worst things to bring about the best things (Romans 8:28). So we trust Him. We trust that He will make our paths straight (Proverbs 3:5-6). We say, *Come what may...we will trust You.* And we know that come what may, He will be faithful. Some will tell us to flee (v1), and some will ask what can the righteous do. And we respond that we will trust Him.

We can boldly say, "If God is for us, who can be against us?" (Romans 8:31). We can be confident that He will use trials to refine us, and that He will bring justice because He is just. And we look forward to the day when we will see His face and dwell in His presence (Psalm 140:13). The trials will be over and we will see and know with everything that we are that we did not trust Him in vain.

We can be confident that He will use trials to refine us

Spend some time thinking about your allegiance to faith and logic. Which do you hold fast to? Does your faith in God triumph over earthly logic?

What does this psalm teach you about what the Lord despises? How does this expand your understanding of who God is?

What does this psalm teach you about what the Lord loves? Does this psalm encourage you to flee from sin and unrighteousness?

His Word Will Never Fail

WEEK THREE

DAY TWO

Psalm 12

We are weak, but He is strong. We are faithless, but He is faithful. In this psalm of David, David laments that the faithful remnant is dwindling. The scene he described does not sound much different than our own day with people lying, flattering, and celebrating sin. This psalm contrasts man's words with God's Word. Man speaks lies and lifts themselves up, covering their sin. They speak flattery that manipulates people and situations.

God's faithful people may find themselves in suffering, but verse 5 reminds us that God hears the oppression of the needy. God hears the affliction of His people like a prayer without words. He sees what we are facing, even when we feel as though we have no strength to even pray. And at just the right moment, He will come. He will arise and come to our rescue, and He will give us rest and safety. Our God will arise for us. He will make us secure and fulfill our longings. Man's words will fail, but God's Word will never fail us. His words are pure. His words have been tried and tested and have proved true time and time again. *His words will never fail. Man's words are weak, His Word is strong. Man's words lie, His Word is truth. Man's words wound, His Word heals.*

When the words of this world fail us, we can run to His Word that will never fail. Life in this world is difficult, but we can take heart because He has already overcome the world (John 16:33). In a world that is against us, our God is for us.

Life in this world is difficult, but we can take heart because He has already overcome the world

Reread verses 3-4. What do these verses tell you about the power of our words?

Meditate on verse 6. Do you love the Lord's words? Do you trust them to be true and pure and beautiful?

Focus on the last two verses of this psalm. How does it comfort you to know that the Lord guards His people despite being surrounded by the wicked?

He Has
Dealt
Bountifully
with Me

WEEK THREE

DAY THREE

Psalm 13

How often we have found ourselves in a situation where our feelings do not line up with the truth. David finds himself in that position in this psalm. The psalm likely was written while David was running from Saul, and the beginning of the psalm shows us what David felt. At the start of the psalm we see David feeling forgotten. It seems like the Lord is far away and that God had hidden Himself. It is easy for us to feel this way in the midst of our trials. But the Lord had made a promise with David, and He would not forsake it (2 Samuel 7). David cried out to the Lord for Him to consider or look on him and to answer. David was desperate to be heard by the Lord. David wanted to be rescued for his own sake as well as for the sake of God's name and glory.

And then in verse 5 the psalm shifts, and suddenly we go from what David was feeling to what David knew. His fear had been turned to faith. David triumphantly declared that He was trusting in God's steadfast love. He was placing his faith in the covenant keeping *Hesed* love of God, and he was confident that God would keep His Word. He rejoiced in God's salvation and praised God who had dealt bountifully with him. The Hebrew word here for "bountifully" is *gamal*. It shows that God had been good and dealt bountifully, but it also has the idea of ripening like fruit. You see, David's circumstances hadn't changed, but God was changing him, growing him, and ripening him. God was dealing bountifully with him.

Our situation doesn't always change, and God never changes, but He changes *us*. He grows us and ripens us. He helps us to see His goodness and love for us even when life doesn't go as planned. So will God forget us? Never! We are His children and He will never forget us (Isaiah 49:15-16). He will never forget us, but He will grow us so that even in the midst of suffering we will be able to see His faithfulness and steadfast love for us. May we never allow our feelings to dictate our theology, but allow our theology to dictate our feelings. He has dealt bountifully with us.

But I have trusted in your faithful love; my heart will rejoice in your deliverance. I will sing to the Lord because he has treated me generously.

Psalm 13:5-6

Do you sometimes find yourself with the same feelings of being forsaken that David felt? How does the end of this psalm encourage you when your feelings do not line-up with the truth?

In what ways does David's confidence in the Lord amid trials grow your ability and desire to praise the Lord while experiencing difficulty?

Think about what "bountiful" means. How does this psalm challenge your views about what is good and bountiful for us?

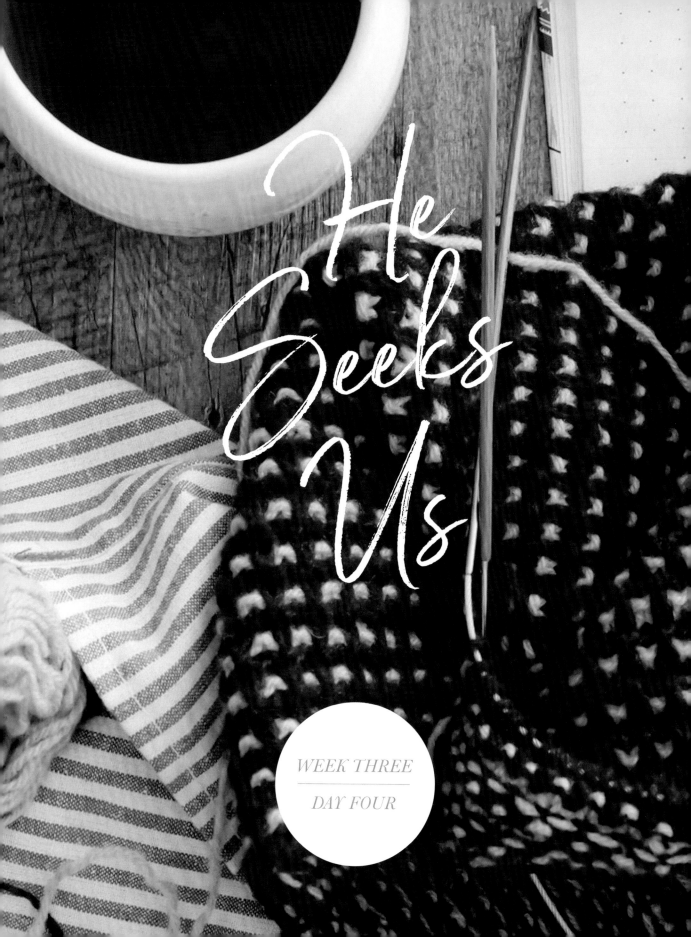

He Seeks Us

WEEK THREE

DAY FOUR

Psalm 14

This psalm has often been called a psalm on practical atheism. The foolish say in their hearts that there is no God, and men are so prone to live as if there is no God. We think that we know what is best for ourselves, and we often exalt ourselves to the place of God in our own hearts and lives. This psalm shows the condition of every man, and Paul quotes much of it in Romans 3 as he describes the human condition apart from God. In ourselves we can do nothing good (John 15:5), and even the good things we do are often done with skewed motives.

But the Lord changes everything. In ourselves we do not seek the Lord, but praise God that He sought us and loved us first (1 John 4:19, Romans 5:8). He loved us while we were unlovable, and He paid for our salvation while we were still the enemies of God. This psalm does not end without the sweet hope of Jesus. We make such a mess of our lives, and yet Jesus is our great hope. He does what we could never do. He loved us while we were still sinners and has exchanged our sin for His righteousness (2 Corinthians 5:21).

This world is full of sin and suffering, but there will come a day when sin and suffering will be no more and our God will restore and redeem everything. He will free us from the captivity of this world and restore us fully to Himself as He defeats sin and death forever and restores His people. For now we wait with expectation because we know that He will not make us wait a moment too long. We will praise Him in the waiting.

Jesus is our great hope

Go and read John 15:5. In what ways do you see the precepts of this verse throughout Psalm 14?

Think about your life before you accepted Christ. Did your former life resemble the character traits found in this psalm?

As you meditate on this chapter, are you encouraged to seek after the Lord more fervently?

Hear His Heart

WEEK THREE

DAY FIVE

Psalm 15

Psalm 15 asks, "Who will dwell with the Lord?" It asks this question and then answers it in the verses that follow. This psalm was likely written after the Ark was returned to Jerusalem and David reflected on the joyous occasion. This psalm is the description of the righteous. It is not the way of salvation, but it is the way that the saved should live.

So David asks, *Lord, how do we stay near you? How do we abide with you?* David is seeking the Lord and longing to walk in relationship with Him, and we should desire the same. So who dwells with the Lord? The ones who walk blamelessly and do right. This is not a demand for perfection, but a command for us to live with integrity. This verse, and the whole psalm, is a pleading for us to be more like Jesus who is the only one that perfectly possesses all of these traits. As believers we are constantly in the process of being sanctified and transformed into the image of the Son. So *blamelessness* is a single word that sums up the entire passage. It is not perfection, but integrity before the Lord and before men that God desires from us. It is a tender heart that seeks to serve the Lord and responds to the conviction of the Holy Spirit.

We are to speak truth not just with our lips, but also in our hearts. We must not dwell on lies about others, about ourselves, or about God. We should not use our words to wound or do wrong to those around us. We should honor those that love the Lord and not promote evil. We should keep our word, and deal honestly with our finances. We should live blameless lives not out of duty, but as an overflow of gratitude for the grace we have been given. And the Lord promises that when we are dwelling with Him, we will not be moved. The world around us may shift and change, but we stand firm and unmoved in the grace that we have been given. *We will not be shaken.*

In what ways does this psalm show you how to live with integrity and godliness?

What are some of the attributes/actions listed in this psalm that you struggle with? Spend some time in prayer, asking that God would transform you into Jesus' likeness.

Reread the last line in the psalm. What does it mean to remain unmoved? Do you feel like you are easily shaken or unmovable in your stewardship of God's grace?

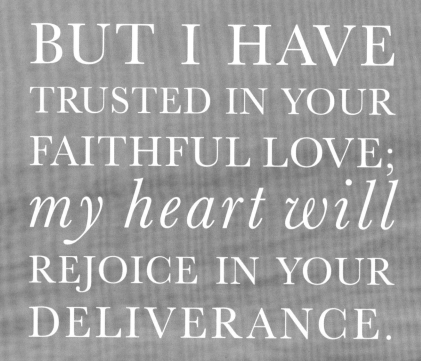

BUT I HAVE TRUSTED IN YOUR FAITHFUL LOVE; *my heart will* REJOICE IN YOUR DELIVERANCE.

Psalm 13:5

WEEKLY REFLECTION

Read Psalms 11-15

- Paraphrase the psalms from this week.

- What did you observe from this week's text about God and His character?

- What do these psalms teach about the condition of mankind and about yourself?

- How do these psalms point to the gospel?

- How should you respond to these psalms? What is the personal application?

- What specific action steps can you take this week to apply the passage?

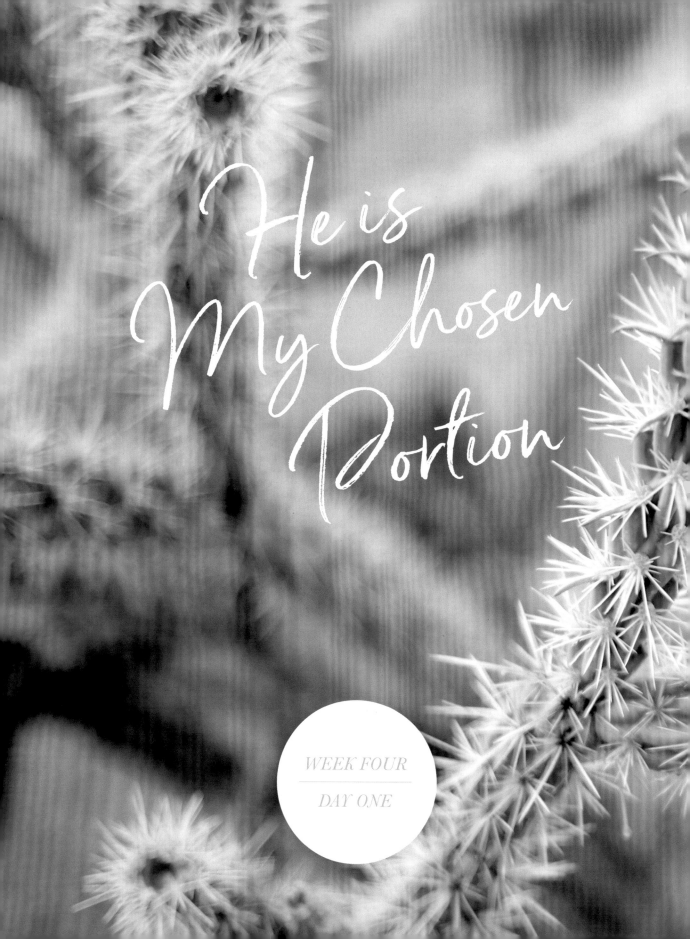

He is
My Chosen
Portion

WEEK FOUR

DAY ONE

Psalm 16

This is a psalm of *joy*. It is not about joy in circumstances but of joy in the Lord. Our joy is not dependent on our circumstances but on who He is. In this psalm, David calls to the Lord who is the one who is with His children. David remembers, and we must as well that all we have is from the Lord, and if we do good it is because of His work in us. As followers of the Lord, we are to love the Lord, love His people, and hate wickedness.

At the center of this psalm, verses 5 and 6 serve as a sweet reminder for us. The wording of these verses refers to the events of the book of Joshua and the boundary lines of the promised land. Each tribe of Israel was given an inheritance, but for the priests and Levites, their inheritance was not land but the Lord Himself. David says that the Lord is his chosen portion. David is saying, and we should as well, *Lord, there is nothing that I want more than You.* The Lord Himself holds our lot, our life is in His hands, and it could not be in a more secure place. Often I am tempted to hold my life myself, but it is so much better for Him to have control. In verse 6, David says that the lines had fallen in pleasant places and that his inheritance was beautiful.

The same is true for us. What the Lord has given us is good, even when we don't understand. His ways are so much better than our ways. David had not been given an easy life, yet still he said that all he had was good. David knew from experience that suffering with the Lord is better than ease without Him. David turned to the Lord night and day, and he found joy in a personal and constant relationship with the Lord. He knew that the Lord was with him, and that was all that he needed. Tucked in verses 9-10 is a prophecy of resurrection and a reminder that it is our Savior that makes this relationship with the Lord a reality to us as believers today.

The psalm ends beautifully with verse 11 and a beautiful declaration of joy. This is a now-and-not-yet promise. Now we see Him lead us in this life, we find joy in His presence, and pleasure in Him. And someday we will see this promise fully fulfilled for us. So for now, we will wait for the Lord who is our chosen portion. We will cling to hope and trust that His plan for us is good. We will say with everything that we are, *Lord, there is nothing we want more than you.*

You reveal the path of life to me;
in your presence is abundant joy;
at your right hand are
eternal pleasures.

Psalm 16:11

What is the difference between having joy in your circumstances or joy in the Lord? Which one will give you lasting satisfaction?

Spend some time in self-examination after reading verse 2. Do you truly understand that our goodness is solely from the Lord?

Meditate on verse 11. How does this verse grow your understanding of the importance of joy in the Lord?

I Will Call Upon the Lord

Psalm 17

The psalms record for us some of the most beautiful prayers ever prayed. David constantly turned to the Lord in prayer, and we can pray these same prayers as well. In this psalm that was likely written while David was on the run from Saul, David cries out to the Lord to hear and answer, and he is confident that God will. At the beginning of the psalm, David comes asking for God to hear his cause after David had searched his heart. We must constantly search our own hearts and motives and align them with God's Word and God's heart. David Guzik paraphrased David's prayer like this, "Lord, I believe my cause is just and I have searched my own heart for deceit. Yet I wait for your vindication, and I want You to do and promote what is right. If I'm not on Your side, move me so that I am." David didn't take matters into his own hands — he asked for the Lord to show up in his circumstances. David also pointed out that it is God's Word that kept him from sin in verse 4. It is Scripture that keeps us from sin as well.

The heart of this psalm is found in verses 6-7. David proclaims that he will call upon the Lord, because the Lord will answer him. David had complete faith and confidence that God would answer his prayer. When we have seen God answer our prayers time and time again, we will come with fresh faith and confidence that He will do it again. Spurgeon said, "He who has tried the faithfulness of God in hours of need, has great boldness in laying his case before the throne." Prayer grows our faith as we see Him prove Himself faithful to us over and over.

David then asks God to show His love. We can come to the Lord boldly and ask Him to wondrously show His wonderful love. David asks to be kept as the apple of God's eye, which connotes being cherished and protected, and then asks to be hidden in the shadow of His wings. This is a place of safety and protection, just as a hen guards her chicks. It also can remind us of the tabernacle and the wings of the cherubim over the Ark of the Covenant. Our God can make even our suffering a holy of holies and a place of communion with Him. His presence is found in the midst of our problems. The psalm ends with a declaration of faith as so many of David's do. David looked to the future, but he also trusted God for the present. This psalm urges us to cry to the Lord in prayer and trust that He will be faithful. Then with David we can say, *Now and forever Lord, You are faithful. You are the only One that satisfies.*

But I will see your face in righteousness; when I awake, I will be satisfied with your presence.

Psalm 17:15

Reread verse 5. What does it mean to have our steps hold fast to the Lord's paths? Spend some time in prayer, asking that God would give you the strength to make your steps hold fast to His paths.

How are verses 6-7 an example of complete faith and confidence in the Lord? In what ways do these verses strengthen your faith in God?

Meditate on verse 15. What does it mean to be satisfied with God's likeness? How can that level of satisfaction bring about complete joy?

He Rescued Me Because He Delighted in Me

Psalm 18

God had promised David that he would be king, and yet Saul chased him. But God was faithful to His promise and would deliver David. Psalm 18 is David's song of praise to our faithful God. The psalm begins with David's declaration of love for the Lord. The Hebrew word for "love" here, *racham*, is very closely related to the Hebrew word for "womb". This love is like a mother's love for her child, tender and compassionate. It is the way God loves us and the way that we should love Him. This plea from David's heart is raw and personal. We do not come to the Lord as one who is far off and disinterested, but as the one who knows us personally, who cares, and will come to our rescue.

In verse 2, David lists so many things that God is and each is prefaced with the word "my." It is a sweet reminder that His love and care is personal to His children. He is my rock and my strength and stability when life is uncertain. He is my fortress and my stronghold, the One that I run to. He is my shield and protection. He is my deliverer and rescuer. He is my horn and my strength. He is my God and I know He will not forsake me. In verse 3, we are reminded that we can walk confidently into any trial because we know that God will be with us. He has been faithful in the past, He will be faithful again. The words of this psalm remind us that God hears the cry and prayers of His people and that He acts on their behalf.

Verse 19 is one of my favorite verses in all of Scripture and is a reminder that He does not rescue us because He has to but because He loves us and delights in us. When we allow this truth to sink into our hearts, our perspective changes. Because David knew of God's love, he could trust even when he didn't understand God's plan. David could confidently proclaim the words of verse 30, that God's ways and timing are perfect, that God's

Word is sure and He always keeps His promises, and that He will rescue His people. Verse 31 asks the question, "Who is God, but the Lord?" It is a reminder that there is none like Him. Nothing satisfies like Jesus. Jonathan Edwards said, "All earthly desires are but streams, but God is the ocean." Even deliverance is not as sweet as the Deliverer. He alone is what our hearts long for. David didn't take matters into his own hands. He waited on the Lord, and he would find that God's ways are so much better than our own.

So in our waiting, we can trust that His way is perfect. We can be confident of His faithfulness and assured of His steadfast love. We can trust Him and know that He is our greatest desire. There is none like Him.

The Lord is my rock, my fortress, and my deliverer, my God, my rock where I seek refuge, my shield and the horn of my salvation, my stronghold.

Psalm 18:2

Reflect on verse 2. Does this verse grow your understanding of God's character? In what ways does this verse comfort you?

In what ways do verses 7-15 illustrate the power and might of the Lord? Why is it important to have a proper understanding of God's power?

Meditate on verse 46. Does it bring you joy to remember that the Lord lives? How might it affect our relationship with God if we do not see Him as living and active?

The Law
of the Lord
is Perfect

Psalm 19

This beautiful psalm shows how God makes Himself known in creation, in His precious Word, and even in our hearts. Our God in grace reveals Himself to us in so many ways. The heavens show His glory, and His Word shows us who He is. The earth shouts out the truth that there is a God and that He is majestic and glorious, and then Scripture introduces Him and shows how He loves us. In the first verses of the psalm, the name for God is "El", which shows His great and majestic power in creation. But when the psalmist speaks of God's Word, the word for God is "Jehovah" or "Yahweh". This is God's covenant name and shows that He is a personal God.

As the psalm goes on, we see the many different functions of God's Word in our lives. God's Word is perfect, and it restores, revives, and refreshes the soul. There is power in the Word of God. God's Word is like water for the thirsty soul. God's Word is living, and it gives life. Scripture is the testimony of the Lord, and it tells us who He is. Who He is changes us and makes us wise. The precepts of the Lord are right, and when we follow the Lord's plan we will live lives of joy. We can have joy when we see that God's ways are the best ways, and we can trust Him even when we don't understand. God's Word is true, trustworthy, and timeless. God's Word opens our eyes and illuminates our path. God's Word is pure. It has been tested and tried. It has stood the test of time and proved faithful, and it will surely prove faithful for us as well. God's Word is powerful and pure, it is enlightening and enduring, it is forever and it is faithful.

There should be nothing that we desire more than God's Word because it is there that we find Him. God's Word is better than all of the possessions one could earn, and it is better than all of the pleasures that this world has to offer. David ends this psalm with recognition of his own weakness and sinfulness and of God's constant faithfulness. God's Word reveals our sin, and then God cleanses us and declares us innocent. We are so easily tempted to sin, but we can be assured that because of God's grace, sin no longer has dominion over us (Romans 6:14). The more we draw near to the Lord, the more we see our own weakness, and the sweeter His grace will be to us.

The psalm ends with a prayer that not only our actions but also our words and the thoughts of our hearts be pure and acceptable before the Lord. "Acceptable" is a term used commonly to refer to the condition of a sacrifice, so here we see our words and thoughts as an offering back to the Lord. We come and give our all to our Rock and our Redeemer who has given all for us. In the heavens above, in His precious Word, and in our hearts, our Redeemer is faithful.

May the words of my mouth
and the meditation of my heart
be acceptable to you, Lord,
my rock and my Redeemer.

Psalm 19:14

Think about verses 7-8. In what ways does the Lord's instruction revive the soul? How does it make us wise? Why does it matter if it's pure?

Meditate on verses 10-11. Why is the Word of God so precious? Does this psalm grow your desire to know God's Word?

Reread verse 14. What are some practical ways that you can challenge the word of your mouth and the meditation of your heart to be pleasing and acceptable to God?

Before We Call, He Will Answer

Psalm 20

Psalm 20 is a song to be sung before battle. The Christian life is often described as a battle, so these words encourage us as we face this life (1 Timothy 6:12, Ephesians 6:12). This is our battle cry. The psalm begins with the people pleading for the Lord to answer in the day of trouble, and verse 6 tells us that He will answer. "Trouble" here means adversity, affliction, distress, and even tightness which give the feeling of being stuck. Haven't we all experienced a day of trouble! The people cry for the name of the Lord to be their protection – and we can as well. The name of the Lord is His Word and His character – it is who He is. We call upon the name and character of God to rescue us as well. The beginning verses are prayers by the people for David before he goes into battle, but many scholars have also viewed this as a prophetic prayer of Jesus before His battle with sin and death on the cross. As children of God we can call on the same God that helped David and the same Father that strengthened Jesus as well.

Verse 4 is a plea for God to grant our heart's desires. As we draw near to the Lord, His will becomes our will. As we constantly abide in Him (John 15), He molds us into His own image and we will desire His will. In verse 6 through the end of the psalm, David answers back with confidence that God will be faithful to His people. The longer we walk with the Lord, and the more we see prayer answered, the more confidence we will have in His faithfulness. Our knowledge will go past just knowing in our heads, to knowing in our hearts that He is faithful. The Hebrew word here means to know by experience. As we see the Lord answer when we call, it gives us confidence to call again. Our God answers His people. David knew that He would answer, and Isaiah 65:24 tells us that He answers before we even call. *He is faithful.*

As they were going into battle, David declared that though some trusted in horses and chariots, God's people would trust in the Lord's name. So often we are tempted to trust in the things we can see, and rest our faith in the tangible. But we can trust in something so much better. The name and character of our God is so much better than anything in this world. The word here for trust means to remember, and when we remember His faithfulness in the past, we can be confident that He will be faithful in the future. We know that the greatest battle has already been won at Calvary, and we know He can handle anything we face in this life. We have confidence in our almighty and faithful God, and we echo the words of Romans 8:31. *If God is for us, who can be against us?*

Some take pride in chariots, and others in horses, but we take pride in the name of the Lord our God.

Psalm 20:7

Read verse 4 and spend some time in self-examination. Are your heart's desires the same as the Lord's? Do you desire His plans?

Reread verses 7-8. In what ways does this passage illustrate the foolishness and frailty that occurs when we hope in earthly things?

Meditate on Romans 8:31. What are some of the ways that this verse describes the same knowledge being displayed through this psalm?

LORD, YOU ARE *MY PORTION* AND MY CUP *of blessing;* YOU HOLD MY FUTURE.

Psalm 16:5

WEEKLY REFLECTION

Read Psalms 16-20

- Paraphrase the psalms from this week.

- What did you observe from this week's text about God and His character?

- What do these psalms teach about the condition of mankind and about yourself?

- How do these psalms point to the gospel?

- How should you respond to these psalms? What is the personal application?

- What specific action steps can you take this week to apply the passage?

We Shall Not Be Moved

WEEK FIVE

DAY ONE

Psalm 21

The 20th psalm was a prayer for victory in battle, and this psalm is a song of praise after that glorious victory. In the Jewish Targum, this psalm of David was originally known as the "Psalm of King Messiah." It shows David as a type or picture of Christ, with Jesus as the ultimate and full fulfillment of the words of this psalm. This is a psalm of praise to the Lord for His faithful deliverance. Warren Wiersbe said that "answered prayers ought to be acknowledged by fervent praise." That is exactly what this psalm does. It pours out praise to the God who is faithful. We should praise Him for who He is and for what He does. He is faithful and good, and everything that He does is faithful and good.

The psalm details all the ways the Lord was faithful, and we would be wise to name His faithfulness in our lives and let it remind us to trust Him for the future. The Lord had given His people their heart's desire. The beauty of walking with the Lord is that the more we grow in Him and align our hearts with His heart, the more our hearts will desire His will. Verse 3 says that He meets with rich blessings. The word here for "meet" means "to go before." Our God goes before us, and we can have confidence in that truth no matter what we are facing in this life. With the Lord with us and before us, we will not be moved.

This life is full of battles, but our Savior and Warrior has already overcome on the cross. We can go ahead confidently into battle because He goes before us, and He is with us. We can trust that the day will come when all in this world will be made right. The victory of Jesus our Messiah gives us confident faith that just as He has been faithful in the past, He will be faithful again. So we will praise His name and know that there is victory in the name of Jesus. We can remember His faithfulness and pray for Him to do it again.

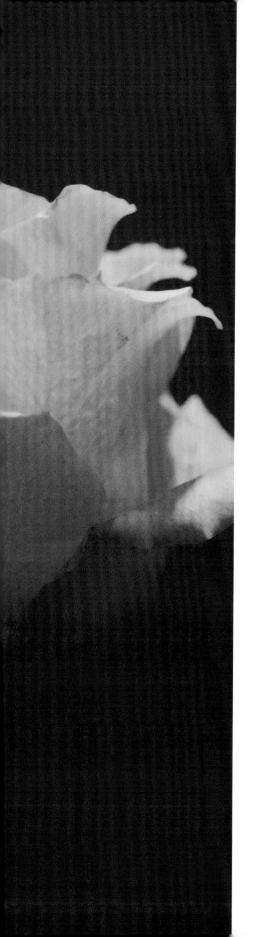

After reading through this psalm, what are some of the ways that you see it point to Christ?

Verse 11 reminds us that plans to thwart God will not succeed. How can this give you encouragement in your everyday life? Do you trust in the Lord's plans?

How does this psalm illustrate the confidence we can have going into the battles of life? In what ways does it grow your affection toward the Lord to know He goes before us?

Psalm of
the Cross

WEEK FIVE

DAY TWO

Psalm 22

The 22nd psalm has been called the psalm of the cross. This strikingly beautiful psalm practically speaks of Jesus in vivid detail. In a small sense, perhaps it shows the suffering of David, but it is without a doubt a psalm about the Son of David. The psalm contains many direct quotes of what Jesus said on the cross, and it is possible that He recited this while on the cross. The psalm begins with the Messiah crying out to the Lord. On the cross, the weight of our sin was placed on the spotless Son of God which caused the Father to look away and forsake the Son for a time. This is the great exchange, or the holy transaction. He took our sin so that we could take His righteousness (2 Corinthians 5:21). Yet even in His suffering, the Messiah would proclaim the holiness of Jehovah. Jesus knew that God had a holy plan, and that His ways are always good. No matter how bad things seem to be, we know that God is holy. And sometimes it is the very worst things in life that bring the very best things. The cross teaches this truth that our God can use anything for His glory and the good of His people.

The psalm continues with a detailed description of the suffering of our Savior. Verse 14 shows Jesus expressing that He is poured out, and our hearts take pause at the weight of the Living Water poured out for us. Verse 16 tells of His pierced hands and feet. David is prophetically describing the crucifixion. He had probably never seen a crucifixion as this was not a Jewish practice, and even the Romans would not begin the practice for hundreds of years. But God's plan had been set in place before the ages began. Verse 17 tells us each bone was visible and not broken as prophesy has foretold (Psalm 34:20), and as a beautiful fulfillment of Jesus as our perfect Passover lamb (Exodus 12:46, Numbers 9:12). They stared and they mocked our Savior, but now we gaze on the same Savior with gratitude and praise.

The tone of the psalm shifts at verse 21 as we shift from sorrow to joy. Because it is the sorrow of the cross that brings hope and joy to all. Our Jesus has gone to the cross to glorify the Father, and because of His great love for us. He has done what we could never do on our own. The agony of the cross gives way to the triumph of the resurrection and the joy of salvation. The psalm ends with the reminder that *it is finished*. He has done it. Our Redeemer has paid the price for us and now He lives.

All the ends of the earth will remember and turn to the Lord. All the families of the nations will bow down before you

Psalm 22:27

Think about the similarities between this psalm and Jesus' time on the cross. What does this foretelling display about the nature and character of God? Why might Jesus' recitation of this psalm on the cross be important?

Meditate on verse 26. In what ways does this verse give you hope?

How does the shift in this psalm from sorrow to joy help you to understand the way in which we should remember Jesus' sacrifice for us?

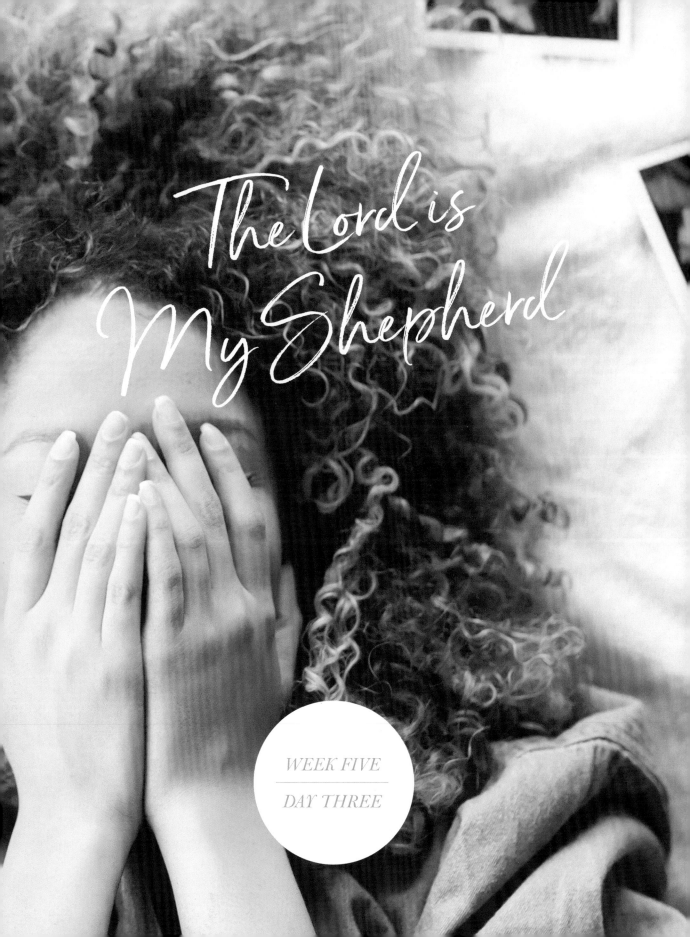

The Lord is My Shepherd

WEEK FIVE
——
DAY THREE

Psalm 23

This psalm is one of the most well known portions of Scripture, but I pray that we will not allow it's familiarity to lessen the utter beauty of it. Its fame is for good reason, and there is perhaps no portion of Scripture that has comforted more people than this one. It begins with those famous words, "The Lord is my Shepherd." Our Sovereign God has chosen to shepherd His people. The image is seen throughout the Old Testament (Genesis 48:15, 49:24, Ps. 28:9, 80:1, 95:7, 100:3, Is. 40:11), and Jesus would declare in John 10 that *He* is the Good Shepherd. He is *my* Shepherd because this relationship is intimate and personal. Not just *a* shepherd or even *the* shepherd, but He is *mine*. I shall not want because with Jesus I have all that I need.

He makes me lie down and leads me beside still waters. The Hebrew here is literally "waters of rest." He gives rest to my soul, and then He restores my soul. He restores, or refreshes, and revives my soul. He doesn't have to change my circumstances to give me peace. I have peace because He is with me. I am refreshed by the water of His Word each time I come to Him. He leads me in the way I should go for my good and for His glory. As the tone shifts in this psalm, we are reminded that following the Lord does not mean there will never be difficulty. But we face just the shadow of death, because death was defeated on the cross as we learned in Psalm 22. Because He is with us, we have nothing to fear. He comforts and disciplines us with His rod and staff, and we can know He will come tenderly with conviction when we stray. Then right in the midst of our troubles and our enemies, He will prepare a banquet for us and give us peace and rest. Because when we stay near our Shepherd we can have peace and joy right in the midst of trouble. Our peace is dependent on God alone and is unchanged by the circumstances around us. He gives us fresh anointing and fills our lives until they overflow.

The psalm ends with the sweet reminder of God's constant goodness and His steadfast love. The word "surely" means "only". And someday we will look back on our lives and see only God's goodness and steadfast *hesed* love. Because when we finally see our life from His perspective, we will see that even our trials were goodness, mercy, and steadfast love. Someday, we will dwell in His house and praise Him as we see all that He has been for us. He has been our guide, our rest, our comfort, our protector, our correction, our joy, and our Lord. He is our Shepherd, and we are His sheep.

When the soul grows sorrowful, he revives it; when it is sinful he sanctifies it; when it is weak he strengthens it.
-Charles Spurgeon

Only goodness and faithful love will pursue me all the days of my life, and I will dwell in the house of the Lord as long as I live.

Psalm 23:6

How does Jesus' proclamation that He is the good shepherd testify to His oneness with the Father? Why is this important?

Why is it important to understand Jesus as our shepherd? Why is it important to understand ourselves as His sheep?

Meditate on the comfort that is offered to us through this psalm and repeat it in prayer to God.

The King of Glory

Psalm 24

Psalm 24 is a triumphant song about our King of Glory. It was likely written to be sung at the entrance of the Ark of the Covenant into Jerusalem (2 Samuel 6, 1 Chronicles 15:1-16:3). The psalm begins with the declaration that the earth is the Lord's and so are all who dwell on earth (Galatians 3:28). The psalmist then asks the question of who will ascend the hill of the Lord. The Christian life is often described as a journey or as going higher with the Lord. We long to go higher with Him and to know Him more and more. So who is it that goes higher with Him? The psalmist says it is those that have clean hands and a pure heart. Clean hands in this passage refer to our actions – this is the way that we live. A pure heart refers to our motives and our heart attitudes. It is easy to fall into the trap of doing the right things with self-serving motives, but we are urged to have not only clean hands but a pure heart as well.

The psalmist then points us to the only One that makes right living and a pure heart possible. Our gaze is shifted to the King of Glory Himself. Right living and pure motives are only possible through Jesus and His grace. He takes our sin and our selfish hearts and clothes us in His own righteousness (2 Corinthians 5:21). This is the beauty of the gospel. This psalm is thought by many to be something that would go back and forth. The question would be asked, "Who is this King of Glory?" And the people would answer, "The Lord, strong and mighty." So the question is posed at the beginning of the psalm of who can be near the Lord, and then we are shown that the one that has been perfect in our place. The One with a pure heart and clean hands is Jesus Himself. And our hearts and hands are made clean because we are in Him. We praise our King of Glory for being righteous for us.

He takes our sin and our selfish hearts and clothes us in His own righteousness

Spend some time in self-examination regarding verse 4. Why is it important to have clean hands and a pure heart? What does it look like to lift our souls up to what is false?

Think about the answer to the question, "who is the King of glory?" Who do you say the King of glory is? How does this psalm direct your thoughts in understanding the Lord?

Read 2 Corinthians 5:21. How does knowing that at the time this psalm was written the Israelites were required to practice offerings and sacrifices to maintain purity grow your understanding of Jesus as the perfect sacrifice?

Teach Me Your Path

WEEK FIVE

DAY FIVE

Psalm 25

This psalm is a passionate plea from the heart of David to the Lord. He comes to the Lord as the One to whom he lifts his soul – a reminder to us that our God should be the place that we run to. There is no one else who will bring peace to our hearts. *Even when life does not make sense, I will turn in prayer to You and trust You.* Throughout the psalm we see the psalmist waiting on the Lord, but he declares in verse 3 that none that wait for the Lord will be put to shame. This world may try to make us feel foolish for trusting our God, but we can be confident that our God will never fail us.

David came to the Lord is prayer in verse 1, and in verses 4-5 we see him turning to God's Word. It is on the pages of God's Word that we find His direction and will for our lives. As we wait on the Lord we can draw near to Him in prayer and pour out our hearts. *We can seek Him through His Word.* David goes on to proclaim the character of God. He is again coming to the Lord to plead God's character on his behalf. We can do the same as we come to Him in prayer. He has always been faithful to us. Spurgeon said, "There shall be mercy in every unsavory morsel, and faithfulness in every bitter drop." Everything God does is an evidence of His faithfulness because that is who He is. We do not always understand His ways, but we can trust that as we are following Him, even the things that seem bitter to us are mercies and faithfulness that we do not understand.

Finding God's will is about daily following the Lord, seeking Him continually, and trusting Him to direct my steps. Verse 15 reminds us to constantly set our gaze to the Lord and wait for Him. We can be confident that He will be faithful to us.

Guide me in your truth and teach me,
for you are the God of my salvation;
I wait for you all day long.

Psalm 25:5

Do you find that you often will first run to the Lord when you are distressed? In what ways does this psalm instruct and encourage you to seek God in prayer?

Reflect on verses 4-5. Do you desire to know the Lord's ways? Do you aspire to be led by His truth? Spend some time in prayer, praying these verses to God.

What are some practical ways that you can follow the Lord daily, seek Him continually, and trust Him to direct your steps?

BE EXALTED, LORD, *IN YOUR STRENGTH;* WE WILL SING AND PRAISE *YOUR MIGHT.*

Psalm 21:13

WEEKLY REFLECTION

Read Psalms 21-25

- Paraphrase the psalms from this week.

- What did you observe from this week's text about God and His character?

- What do these psalms teach about the condition of mankind and about yourself?

- How do these psalms point to the gospel?

- How should you respond to these psalms? What is the personal application?

- What specific action steps can you take this week to apply the passage?

I Love
Your House

WEEK SIX

DAY ONE

Psalm 26

In this psalm, David begins by begging the Lord for vindication and ends the psalm with shouts of praise. David faced many trials in his life and had many people close to him go up against him. But verse 1 tells us that he had trusted the Lord without wavering. Oh may the same be said of us! Spurgeon said, "Confidence in God is a most effectual security against sin." When we are trusting the Lord it keeps us constantly near Him, away from sin, and able to trust that God is working all things for our good (Romans 8:28).

David also asked the Lord to prove and try or examine him. David was seeking to live a holy life and then asking the Lord to examine his heart and mind. David said in verse 3 that God's steadfast love was before his eyes. As we remember God's great love and kindness toward us, it should lead us to holiness and repentance (Romans 2:4). His grace should not give us a license to sin, but His grace should compel us to holiness and to praise (Romans 6:1-2). David points out that he did not sit with wicked or vain men. We are reminded of the importance of the people that we spend time with. It has been said that we become like the people that we spend the most time with, and we should seek out relationships that point us to the Lord.

This is also when David speaks about His love for God's house. As believers we should love the church. Matthew Henry said, "Those who have communion with God, and delight in approaching Him, find it (the church) to be a constant pleasure, a comfortable evidence of their integrity, and a comfortable earnest of their endless felicity." Matthew Henry in the last phrase is essentially claiming that the church should be a down payment of heaven to the believer. The church is an imperfect glimpse of the perfect reality of heaven. Someday we will worship the Lord there with the saints of every nation and every age, and the church today is a glimpse as we worship in diverse unity. For now, until that day, we will praise our Savior here and worship Him for who He is while we wait for His return.

But I live with integrity;
redeem me and be gracious to me.
My foot stands on level ground;
I will bless the Lord in the
assemblies.

Psalm 26:11-12

What might it look like to walk with integrity and trust the Lord without wavering? Why is it important to do so?

Reread verse 4-5. Why should we continually examine who we fellowship with? Why is it crucial to surround yourself with other believers?

What does it mean to love the habitation of the Lord's house, as stated in verse 8? Why should we dwell so closely to the Lord?

I Will Seek You

WEEK SIX

DAY TWO

Psalm 27

No matter what is happening in our lives, whatever situation we may find ourselves in, we can trust in the Lord. In this psalm, David speaks of his confidence in the Lord. We know that David's life was not always easy, and yet still he trusted the Lord. David knew in his soul that with God on his side, he had nothing to fear (Romans 8:3). We need not ever fear or worry about what might happen or the foes that are against us. So often we are prone to worry about what could happen, but David tells us that we have nothing to fear.

David then shifts his focus in verses 4-6 with what Wiersbe says is equal to the New Testament concept of abiding in Christ (John 15). Our hearts should desire and seek after the Lord. We should long to dwell, or abide, with Him and to gaze on Him, meditating on who He is. Verse 5 reminds us that we should desire Him and seek after Him because He will be faithful to us. He will be our shelter even when our situation seems hopeless. As the Lord asks all of His people to seek Him, our individual hearts echo back to Him that we will do His will. If He has told us to seek, we will seek. If he has told us to go, we will go. And if He has told us to wait, we will wait. The word here for "seek" in Hebrew is *baqash* and can mean "to seek, to find." It is a sweet reminder that when we seek Him, we will find Him (Jeremiah 29:13). This should be the cry of our hearts that "I will seek you." And we can have full confidence that we *will* find Him.

David ends the psalm with the passionate declaration that he knows that God will be faithful to him. We can live with that same confidence that our God will be faithful to us. So whatever situation we find ourselves in, we can confidently wait on the Lord, knowing that He will be faithful. We expect and await and look eagerly for Him because we know that He will never fail us.

What does verse 4 reveal about what David found the most valuable? Do you also find that you desire and value dwelling with the Lord and appreciating His beauty?

Meditate on verse 14. Why is it important to wait on the Lord and remain strong and courageous in so doing?

Do you find it challenging to wait on the Lord and trust Him? As you reflect on this psalm, spend some time in prayer, asking that God would strengthen your faith and trust in His timing.

In Him My Heart Trusts

Psalm 28

Delay does not mean defeat. Just because the Lord has us in a season of waiting does not mean that He is not working. *He is working in the waiting.* In this psalm, David cries to the Lord and pleads with the Lord to hear and be faithful to him. It is to the Lord alone that we cry out, because we know that He will listen. And after He has listened, and in His timing, we can be sure that He *will* act.

We reflect with David about where we would be without the Lord, and we take comfort that He is with us. We plead with Him to hear, and then we lift up our empty hands to Him. Spurgeon says, "We lift up empty hands for we are beggars; we lift them up because we seek heavenly supplies; we lift them toward the mercy seat of Jesus, for there our expectation dwells." Our God is our only hope, so we come to Him with expectation. We look at the situation we are in, no matter how bad it may be, and then we look expectantly for just a glimpse of how He is already working. We *know* He is working, so we search for that glimmer of His grace right in our mess. Like watching a pot of water about to boil, it sometimes seems we wait so long, but sure enough every pot of water on a hot stove will boil, and every situation in our lives will be an evidence of grace. So we wait with anticipation for those first bubbles to rise to the surface as a sweet reminder that He is working.

As the psalm moves on, we see God's justice over wickedness. Right now we plead for God's mercy on men, but someday we will also be comforted by His justice over sin. Then David's prayer turns to praise. It is the kind of praise made rich by seeing and experiencing God's steadfast love and faithfulness through the years. Our God is our strength and our shield, our protector. In verse 7, we see that as we place our trust in Him we are helped.

First we trust, and then we triumph. The psalm ends with David pleading God's character — and we can do the same. We acknowledge and praise God for who He is and then ask Him to do it for us. David turned his problems into prayer and his prayers into praise. *Oh that we would do the same.*

The Lord is my strength and my shield; my heart trusts in him, and I am helped. Therefore my heart celebrates, and I give thanks to him with my song.

Psalm 28:7

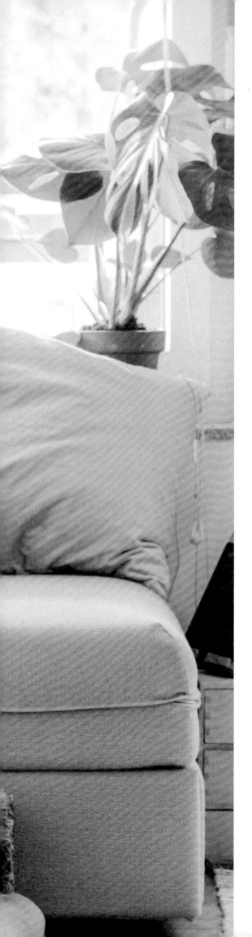

Reflect on the very first line of this psalm. Do you make it a habit to call on the Lord in prayer? Why is this an important discipline in the Christian life?

What does it look like for us to know that the Lord is our strength and shield? How does this change the way we experience difficulty and trials?

In the last line we see the Lord referred to as a shepherd. How does this psalm expand your understanding of the analogy that God is our shepherd and we are His sheep?

Sing in the Star

WEEK SIX

DAY FOUR

Psalm 29

The child of God can sing in the storm. No matter what may come, we can praise Him. The psalm opens with the call to ascribe to the Lord *glory*. With the angels above, we are called to pour out our worship to our God. We are called to give Him the glory due His name. Our mortal tongues could never fully give Him the worship that He deserves, so we pour out our worship as best as we can and as often as we can. As we grow in holiness, we are constantly seeking to take our eyes off ourselves and fix our eyes on Him. All of nature proclaims His praise, and even the storms of this life proclaim His majesty.

In nature and in Scripture, God's voice is powerful. His Word has the power to change, comfort, encourage, convict, and bring to life. Nature points to our God and should produce worship from His people. Even after the thunder and the storm, if the flood waters come, He is not alarmed because He is in control of it all. The child of God can sing in the storm because we know the master of the storm. The master of the storm brings peace to the storm and peace to our hearts. The thunders of the storms of this life will only turn our hearts to the thunder of His voice. It is Him alone who calms the hearts of His people, who give strength to their souls, and who fills them with His peace. He gives us *shalom* peace right in the midst of the storm. He gives us confidence in who He is. *We give Him glory, and He gives us peace.* He gives us strength and peace because He gives us Himself – and that is all we will ever need.

His Word has the power to change, comfort, encourage, convict, and bring to life.

Look up the definition for the word "ascribe."
How does this definition help you understand this psalm?

In what ways does this chapter grow your understanding
of the power of God? How does this description of
God's voice grow your understanding of the power
within the Word of God, our Bibles?

Meditate on verse 10. Why is it important for us to
remember the Lord on His throne?

Joy Comes in the Morning

WEEK SIX

DAY FIVE

Psalm 30

Glory to thee for all the grace I have not tasted yet.
-Charles Spurgeon

This beautiful psalm of David is titled as a song at the dedication of the temple. It would be easy to skip over this title, but it holds great significance because David had passed away at the time the temple was dedicated, but God had promised him that Solomon his son would complete it. This is a song of faith to a faithful God. David knew that God would be faithful, so he wrote this psalm as if it had already happened. What an example to us to start praising Him even before we see the fulfillment of His promises because we know that He will be faithful.

In this psalm, David reminds us that he had faced much difficulty. Foes had come against him, and his own sin and despair had caused him to walk through some dark days. But the Lord was there every step of the way. David lifted God up because God had lifted David up. David lifted the Lord up in praise because God had lifted David up out of despair. The psalm proclaims the theme that our weeping and sorrow and trouble will last for but a moment. The night will not last forever, and morning will break through just like the power of God's grace and mercy in our lives. Jesus Himself would speak much the same words in John 16:20 when He promised the disciples that He would turn, or transform, their sorrow into joy. *That is the power of resurrection.* In pride David had once thought that he would never be moved, as we so often do, but God in His mercy would do what was best for David and for us as well.

He allows us to face both weeping and joy because He knows what is best for us. Someday we will be able to look back on our lives and say "Only goodness and mercy" just as David did in Psalm 23. *Because our God uses everything for our good (Romans 8:28).* Our mourning will be turned to dancing, our sackcloth will be exchanged for gladness, and our hearts will respond in praise to Him. The little word "that" at the beginning of verse 12 reminds us of the purpose even in our suffering. We are going to face suffering, and He is going to be faithful. There will be dark nights, but the sun will surely rise. And it will all happen "so that" everything we are will praise Him. We will see Him in our suffering and be utterly convinced that His faithfulness has led us all the way. And like David we can sing and pray these words in faith. *He is faithful.* We know that He will be faithful to us.

You turned my lament into dancing;
you removed my sackcloth
and clothed me with gladness,
so that I can sing to you and not
be silent. Lord my God,
I will praise you forever.

Psalm 30:11-12

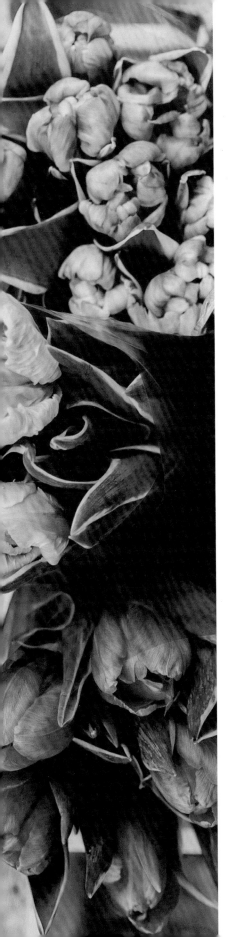

How does the context of this psalm encourage you of God's faithfulness? Are you willing to praise Him and thank Him for what He's done, even if you haven't seen the full picture?

Meditate on verse 11. In what ways has the Lord turned your own mourning into dancing?

Now that we have finished studying the first thirty psalms, reflect on all that you have learned. What are some of the ways that God has grown your knowledge of Him and of His Word through the Psalms?

THE LORD
IS MY LIGHT
AND MY SALVATION
WHOM SHOULD I FEAR?
THE LORD
IS THE STRONGHOLD
OF MY LIFE
WHOM SHOULD I DREAD?

Psalm 27:1

WEEKLY REFLECTION

Read Psalms 26-30

- Paraphrase the psalms from this week.

- What did you observe from this week's text about God and His character?

- What do these psalms teach about the condition of mankind and about yourself?

- How do these psalms point to the gospel?

- How should you respond to these psalms? What is the personal application?

- What specific action steps can you take this week to apply the passage?

What is the Gospel?

Thank you for reading and enjoying this study with us! We are abundantly grateful for the Word of God, the instruction we glean from it, and the ever-growing understanding about God's character from it. We're also thankful that Scripture continually points to one thing in innumerable ways: the gospel.

We remember our brokenness when we read about the fall of Adam and Eve in the garden of Eden (Genesis 3), when sin entered into a perfect world and maimed it. We remember the necessity that something innocent must die to pay for our sin when we read about the atoning sacrifices in the Old Testament. We read that we have all sinned and fallen short of the glory of God (Romans 3:23), and that the penalty for our brokenness, the wages of our sin, is death (Romans 6:23). We all are in need of grace, mercy, and most importantly—we all need a Savior.

We consider the goodness of God when we realize that He did not plan to leave us in this dire state. We see His promise to buy us back from the clutches of sin and death in Genesis 3:15. And we see that promise accomplished with Jesus Christ on the cross. Jesus Christ knew no sin yet became sin so that we might become righteous through His sacrifice (2 Corinthians 5:21.) Jesus was tempted in every way that we are and lived sinlessly. He was reviled, yet still yielded Himself for our sake, that we may have life abundant in Him. Jesus lived the perfect life that we could not live and died the death that we deserved.

The gospel is profound yet simple. There are many mysteries in it that we can never exhaust this side of heaven, but there is still overwhelming weight to its implications in this life. The gospel is the telling of our sinfulness and God's goodness, and this gracious gift compels a response. We are saved by grace through faith (Ephesians 2:8-9,) which means that we rest with faith in the grace that Jesus Christ displayed on the cross. We cannot save ourselves from our brokenness or do any amount of good works to merit God's favor, but we can have faith that what Jesus accomplished in His death, burial, and resurrection was more than enough for our salvation and our eternal delight. When we accept God, we are commanded to die to our self and our sinful desires and live a life worthy of the calling we have received (Ephesians 4:1).The gospel compels us to be sanctified, and in so doing, we are conformed to the likeness of Christ Himself.

This is hope. This is redemption. This is the gospel.

He made the one who did not know sin to be sin for us, so that in him we might become the righteousness of God.

2 Corinthians 5:21

FOR STUDYING GOD'S
WORD WITH US!

CONNECT WITH US:

@THEDAILYGRACECO

@KRISTINSCHMUCKER

CONTACT US:

INFO@THEDAILYGRACECO.COM

SHARE:

#THEDAILYGRACECO

#LAMPANDLIGHT

WEBSITE:

WWW.THEDAILYGRACECO.COM